T0279861

Lost Attractions
of the
OZARKS

· TIM HOLLIS

THE
History
PRESS

Published by The History Press
Charleston, SC
www.historypress.com

Front cover, top center: John Margolies collection; *top right*: Todd Franklin collection; *bottom*: John Margolies collection.
Back cover: Todd Franklin collection; *insert*: Todd Franklin collection.

Unless otherwise noted, images are courtesy of the author.

First published 2023

Manufactured in the United States

ISBN 9781467152976

Library of Congress Control Number: 2022951583

Notice: The information in this book is true and complete to the best of our knowledge. It is offered without guarantee on the part of the author or The History Press. The author and The History Press disclaim all liability in connection with the use of this book.

There were Goofy Golf courses in widely scattered tourist areas, but they were particularly famous in the resorts along the Gulf Coast. The one in Osage Beach had no known relationship with those, but it did keep an iron grip on its Ozarks identity by presenting mountaineer-themed obstacles, as we shall see in chapter four. *Todd Franklin collection.*

PLACES TO SEE & THINGS TO DO IN

MISSOURI
The Midwest's Greatest Vacationland
HEART OF THE OZARKS COUNTRY

This map from an early 1970s brochure gives us a fairly complete cataloging of the attractions that could be found in the Ozark region during that period. Unlike many tourism promotions, it generously includes some of those across the state line in Arkansas.

CONTENTS

Okay, faithful readers, this is your final warning. If you have an aversion to traditional hillbilly stereotypes such as these, you are advised to turn around and go back right now, because things are only going to get worse from here.

ACKNOWLEDGEMENTS

Although much of the material you will see in the pages that follow originated in my own decades-long collection of memorabilia, credit must be given to the additional sources that enlivened the result. As you will notice in the credit lines for the photos, a number of them (as well as other helpful information) came from fellow tourism collectors and photographers: Bob Cara, Todd Franklin, Starr Johnson, Doug Kirby, Janet McMurrin, Crystal and Leland Payton, Mark Pedro, Donnie Pitchford, Debra Jane Seltzer, Russell Wells and Tim Williams.

We must also acknowledge the late photographer John Margolies, who bequeathed his personal archive to the Library of Congress with the amazing stipulation that no restrictions were to be imposed on its use by other authors and researchers.

No matter where, tourism promoters always latched on to pretty women as a surefire way of attracting certain segments of the population. This smiling duo certainly did their part to ensure that a visit to the Ozarks would be on someone's map, whether in Arkansas or Missouri.

INTRODUCTION

W elcome, friends, to the latest volume in the ongoing "Lost Attractions" series. For those who are new in this neighborhood, perhaps it would be best to begin by explaining the title. Just what is a "lost attraction" of the Ozarks, anyway? Well, it is very simple. A lost attraction can be any type of tourism-related business—roadside attraction, motel, restaurant or other—that no longer exists. Casually flipping through the pages, one might conceivably run across an image and comment, "Hey, that place is still there!" That brings us to the secondary definition: a business that has changed radically over the years and no longer resembles its depiction in vintage photos and postcards, even though technically it may still be operating. Everything clear now?

Now that we have cleared up the first half of the title, let's try to determine what the second half entails. Unlike some other tourist areas, "the Ozarks" has boundaries that are hazy at best and more often nonexistent. The regions that staked their tourism reputations on the Ozarks sometimes strayed far from the actual mountain range of that name. As will be discussed in chapter one, over time, the Ozarks became, in the public's mind at least, more of a subculture than an actual geographic area with boundaries.

So how did we go about deciding just which lost attractions would be included and which were outside our invisible boundary? The southern border was the easiest; that would be the Arkansas River. The large plateau on either side of that waterway separates it from the Ouachita Mountains to the south. That meant Hot Springs and its myriad attractions would be outside the book's scope, since it is technically in the Ouachitas instead of the Ozarks.

The northern boundary of the Ozarks was the biggest problem, but using tourism literature and the way attractions have been promoted over the years led us to conclude that, for this book's purposes, Missouri's Ozarks would occupy roughly the southern third of the state. Drawing a straight line from west to east that includes the Lake of the Ozarks region was the nearest thing to a boundary we could find.

We can truly say that the first real tourism in the Ozarks proper began with the success of Harold Bell Wright's 1907 novel *The Shepherd of the Hills*. Its plot and characters are based on the locals Wright observed during a sojourn in the mountains near Branson, which at that time was barely a wide spot in what was barely a road. Prophetically, in the closing paragraphs of the book, Wright predicts that the coming of the railroad would open up the formerly isolated area to the rest of the world, and he was correct. Add highway construction and soon tourists nationwide were flocking to hunting and fishing facilities in the Branson area, as well as visiting the sites made famous in the book. Of course, we do not have to elaborate on what happened to Branson after that, but somewhat surprisingly the Wright novel, and especially the outdoor drama that was crafted from it, are still vital parts of Branson tourism well over a century after the story was published.

So do not be surprised when the chapters that follow mosey around the hills from central Missouri to northern Arkansas with no visible sense of direction. They (whoever "they" are) say that getting there is half the fun, so this entire tour should be one huge fun-filled frolic. Let's get started!

One

THAR'S GOLD IN THEM THAR HILLBILLIES

Today's young people are totally unfamiliar with the traditional "hillbilly" image made famous by movies, television, cartoons and the tourism industry. There are no doubt many mountain residents who consider that a good thing, but there was indeed a time when the depiction of the lazy, bearded hillbilly with floppy hat and accompanying hound dog was among the most popular graphics of the Ozarks.

That character, of course, was not confined to the Ozarks. It could also be found in the Great Smoky Mountains of Tennessee and even in less traditional hill country areas such as Alabama and South Carolina. But those areas eventually received economic help from the government (the Tennessee Valley Authority is a prime example), while the Ozarks—at least in the public's mind—remained mired in its backwoods backwater, so the hillbilly image persisted.

When Missouri native Paul Henning created *The Beverly Hillbillies* TV comedy in 1962, he was basing the characters on his memories of vacations spent in the Branson area, but he was also careful not to specify the supposed location of their mountain shack. It was not until some six years into the show's run that he had the Clampett clan travel from Beverly Hills "back home" to Silver Dollar City, thus cementing the relationship between the two. Naturally, much mutual promotion ensued.

In this chapter we shall see how various attractions and souvenir companies made use of the hillbilly image. But this isn't the only place it appears. In fact, you will be able to spot hillbilly iconography in practically every chapter that follows. And in chapter two, we will see how the Arkansas side of the Ozarks became home to perhaps the most famous cartoon hillbillies of all.

Ever'body git on th' truck, now!

Old *Matt's Cabin, Shepherd of the Hills*, near Lake Taneycomo

Uncle Matt and Aunt Mollie, Father and Mother of Young Matt

OPPOSITE, TOP: There was a time when hillbilly-themed souvenirs were a vital part of the tourist experience. This is only a tiny selection of items that were produced; some are specific to either Arkansas or Missouri, while others were sold throughout the geographic area the Ozarks covered.

OPPOSITE, BOTTOM & CURRENT PAGE: After Harold Bell Wright's novel *The Shepherd of the Hills* was published in 1907, more tourists began pushing into the area near Branson to see the sites made famous in the book. Wright claimed that the only character in the story based on a real person was postmaster Uncle Ike, but that did not stop other locals from dressing in character and posing for photos and postcards as their chosen namesakes.

Jim Lane's Cabin, Shepherd of the Hills, near Lake Taneycomo

As for Uncle Ike, his real-life counterpart, Lee Morrill, spent the rest of his life greeting *Shepherd* fans at his post office, officially designated as Notch, Missouri. This folder was postmarked by Morrill in 1926. Eight years later, the Notch post office was decommissioned by the government, but the building recently underwent restoration by the Shepherd of the Hills Farm attraction in Branson.

Perhaps no *Shepherd of the Hills* character inspired as many tourism promoters as its leading lady, Sammy Lane. This postcard hardly fits the description of Sammy as given in Wright's text (which makes her sound very much like a distant ancestor of Elly May Clampett), but it remained on sale for many years.

By the time of this 1941 view of the bridge leading into Branson—yes, believe it or not, that's how it looked—Sammy Lane's name had been applied to a tourist camp with all the amenities that could be expected in that time and place. For those who have missed the information, man-made Lake Taneycomo was named after its location in Taney County, MO (Missouri).

Perhaps the strangest tie-in with the *Shepherd* characters was the Sammy Lane Adventure Cruise, in which the excursion boat was attacked by pirates. Even Harold Bell Wright never thought of that as a plot element in his story. Branson also had an Old Matt's Motel that looked more like a Holiday Inn than anything in the Wright novel.

OPPOSITE, TOP: It took until 1960 for *The Shepherd of the Hills* to be turned into a drama performed in an outdoor amphitheater. Once that happened, a mini–theme park grew up around it, although at the time of this early brochure, it was still a rather simple attraction. Today's Shepherd of the Hills Farm still has these basic elements but has grown to include various types of amusement rides and other activities.

OPPOSITE, BOTTOM: By far the most common hillbilly image in tourism was the bewhiskered old-timer with his long rifle always at the ready. Accessories such as hound dog, moonshine jug and outhouse were optional.

Second only to the whiskery old coot was the fetching mountain lass wearing as little clothing as the designers could manage without getting arrested. This Arkansas decal plays on the title of a song from the Broadway musical *Annie Get Your Gun*.

OPPOSITE, TOP: In contrast to the cartoon hillbillies, this 1939 Arkansas postcard comes across as positively elegant. The house pictured in the letter *O* was the Van Buren home of famed rural radio comedian Bob Burns, who gained fame for his anecdotes about his rustic relatives—not always welcomed by the folks back home.

OPPOSITE, BOTTOM: Of course, real life was not nearly as comical as cartoon hillbillies and country comedians made it out to be. We can feel nothing but sympathy for this Ozark family, especially since they likely received little or no compensation for having their photo mass-produced by the thousands on postcards.

Hillbilly Home and Family in the Ozarks

By contrast, this family made a good living from posing for postcards and calendars. Bruce Seaton worked for both Silver Dollar City and the *Shepherd of the Hills* drama and saw potential in staging these scenes using his own brood. Noticeably, they avoided the usual scanty attire for the female family members; otherwise, the men and boys fit firmly into the expected stereotype.

The construction of Bagnell Dam in 1931 created Lake of the Ozarks. Dozens of resorts evolved along its miles of coastline, but most of the attractions of the type documented in this book were clustered along US Highway 54. Hundreds of miles from any genuine beachfront property, communities such as Osage Beach stepped up their game to become hubs of tourist activity.

OPPOSITE, TOP: Just because Lake of the Ozarks was nowhere near Branson or northern Arkansas did not mean it was going to be left out of the great hillbilly stakes. In the 1970s, Ollie Osage did his part to advertise Osage Beach and its attractions, but he did not survive the decline of cartoon hillbillies in the years that followed. *Todd Franklin collection.*

LEFT: In Arkansas, Eureka Springs was generally a more elegant and upscale mountain resort than the ones on the Missouri side of the state line, but in this 1956 brochure even highfalutin Eureka couldn't resist bringing in the moonshiner and his still as a way of plugging its Ozark locale.

OPPOSITE, BOTTOM: Around 1980, photographer John Margolies was traveling through the Ozarks when he found this billboard a half mile from Willow Springs, Missouri. He obviously found the typical hillbilly iconography worth preserving. *John Margolies collection.*

HILLBILLY MARKET

Hwy. 71 South—Rt. 1
ROGERS, ARKANSAS 72756

"A slice of country ham
packed between two slices
of bread make a meal
fit for a king."

Telephone:

Days—ME 6-4590
Nights—ME 6-4591

OPPOSITE, TOP: Back to the Arkansas side of the Ozarks, this Hillbilly Market undoubtedly filled a need for tourists passing through Rogers. Attempts to learn more about it, or even when it closed, have come to naught. Such is the lack of permanence in the ever-changing tourism industry.

OPPOSITE, BOTTOM: Perhaps the legendary Route 66 was responsible for bringing more travelers into the Ozarks than any other highway. It sliced its way through Missouri from St. Louis to Joplin, and the sheer novelty of driving through the hill country was enough for tourists headed from Chicago to California, who found it charmingly exotic.

ABOVE: In Missouri, the path of Route 66 was eventually replaced by that of I-44. Where pieces of the old highway still exist, they have often been designated as historic sites. This patch of ancient Route 66 pavement at Rolla, photographed in 2017, seems to be fading into oblivion. *Russell Wells collection.*

TOP: The collection of businesses at Booger Hollow, Arkansas ("Population 7, countin' one hound dog"), barely qualified for this book. Situated near Russellville, they were only a few miles north of the Arkansas River that forms the southern boundary of the Ozark country. While Booger Hollow still exists as a township, the tourist attraction operated only from 1961 to 2004.

BOTTOM: Back at Lake of the Ozarks, a simulated town was named Dogpatch, after the locale of the *Li'l Abner* comic strip, even though the attraction's owners never licensed the cartoon characters or anything else directly referencing the strip. This early postcard puts the emphasis on its Reptile Gardens, a brand of attraction we shall revisit in chapter five.

Dogpatch of Lake Ozark still operates, but only as a gigantic gift shop and not as the collection of buildings and mannequins seen here. Now, put on your walking Shmoos and follow us into the next chapter, where we will take an extended look at a far more elaborate—and officially licensed—version of the same Dogpatch concept.

Since Dogpatch of Lake of the Ozarks was not licensed, perhaps we should consider this happy halfwit to be the unlicensed version of Li'l Abner. Actually, this giant hayseed was a lost attraction for several years, but as of this writing, plans are afoot to restore him to his proper place along the US 54 strip. *John Margolies collection.*

Two
A TYPICAL DAY IN DOGPATCH USA

During 1934, the two most famous comic strip hillbillies of all time were introduced to the public. In June, longtime comics star Barney Google inherited property in the North Carolina hills and by autumn had met the individual who would soon take over the whole strip, Snuffy Smith. In August, cartoonist Al Capp began his strip *Li'l Abner*, and soon, its mix of comedy and soap opera made it a hit with readers.

While Snuffy Smith's Hootin' Holler was specifically placed in the Smoky Mountains, the first few *Li'l Abner* strips pinpointed the locale as Dogpatch, Kentucky. Well, let's move ahead about thirty years. By 1967, *Li'l Abner* had been adapted into a bizarre 1940 live-action feature film, an unsuccessful series of animated cartoons, a hit Broadway musical and a Paramount motion picture based on the play. Always looking for the next big thing, when Capp was approached by a group of businessmen from Harrison, Arkansas, about building a *Li'l Abner* theme park in their area, Capp wasted no time telling the press that he had always considered Dogpatch as being in Arkansas. (This did not endear him to certain members of the Arkansas populace.)

Dogpatch USA, as it was named, opened in time for the summer 1968 tourist season. It was never the smashing tourist draw everyone expected—its remote location along a twisting, two-lane highway miles from any other attractions didn't help any—but for quite some time it maintained a prominent place in Ozarks tourism. When Capp chose to end his strip in 1977 and then died two years later, it was the beginning of Dogpatch's "out of sight, out of mind" days. It hung on until after its 1993 season, by which time Capp's characters were long forgotten by the typical demographic for an amusement park.

TOP: The centerpiece of Dogpatch USA was the statue of town founder General Jubilation T. Cornpone, celebrated in a show-stopping musical number in the Broadway play and subsequent Paramount movie adaptation. In this postcard, Abner and Daisy Mae pose with an unusually slim Marryin' Sam.

BOTTOM: Dogpatch USA heavily relied on billboards such as this one to bring in visitors. It sat in an extremely remote location where cars were not likely to be simply passing by and stopping on a whim. "Irregardless," as Mammy Yokum would say, the U.S. post office that had formerly been known as Marble Falls officially changed its name to Dogpatch, Arkansas, in recognition of the park's existence. *John Margolies collection.*

For its first few years, Dogpatch USA could barely have been called an amusement park, as the *Li'l Abner* theming was really its only asset. Like most theme parks, it had a miniature railroad (the West Po'k Chop Speshul), but most other amusements of its type would not have contained a trout farm where tourists could catch their own and have it cleaned on the spot.

As one would expect, the *Li'l Abner* comic strip characters appeared in costumed form roaming the park, but their resemblance to Al Capp's artwork depended on the availability of suitable performers. The park's souvenirs, on the other hand, made full use of the cartoon characters' traditional appearances.

OPPOSITE, TOP: In the comic strip, Broadway show and movie, the female denizens of Dogpatch were traditionally barefoot. That would hardly have been an option for the ladies who had to walk through the park on hot asphalt all day long, so in this publicity shot, note that Daisy Mae has donned more comfortable red sneakers.

OPPOSITE, BOTTOM: Dogpatch, both in the comic strip and in the theme park, had its share of underdressed hillbilly girls. But none of them could come close to this topless toddler pictured on the postcard for the park's petting zoo.

By the time of this 1974 brochure, Dogpatch USA was beginning to look more and more like a traditional theme park. While the artwork was based on Al Capp's original designs, it was not strictly faithful to his concepts. The Yokum family members' eyes look as if they have been imbibing too frequently of that potent local concoction Kickapoo Joy Juice.

AL CAPP'S CHARACTERS COME TO LIFE IN DOGPATCH USA

The whole family will never forget a fun-filled visit with all the famous Al Capp comic characters high up in the beautiful Ozarks. Li'l Abner, Daisy Mae, Mammy and Pappy Yokum, Lonesome Polecat, Hairless Joe and the whole gang are just a-rarin' to meet you in this unusual and exciting world of Dogpatch U.S.A. where you'll double your fun in the neighboring Marble Falls Resort & Convention Center. It all adds up to Twin Parks in the Ozarks — America's most unique year 'round twin park attraction. There's something fun for every one. If thrills turn you on, get set for all kinds of wild and wacky rides like the Brain Rattler, West Po'k Chop Speshul, Antique Car Rides, Monster Mouse, Helicopter, Boat Train

and the Swiss Funicular which takes all visitors down into the valley of Dogpatch. And there's also plenty of entertainment at Komvention Hall and the Western Theater where you'll enjoy a wide variety of musical entertainment hourly. But your fun has just begun. Visit the Animal Farm. Play with the animals. See educated animals perform. Watch the Sea Lions frolic in their own pool. Fish for Rainbow trout. Visit the art and crafts shops. Go horseback riding. Journey down into Dogpatch Caverns deep inside the earth. Browse the many shops and boutiques. Satisfy your taste for good food at several larapin' good eating places. It's a never-never land of clean, mountain fun far from the smog and congestion and maddening pace of modern America. And as long as you decide to visit Dogpatch, plan to stay in one of our motels, your own private chalet or in the rustic Dogpatch Campark, one of America's best, with all hookups and conveniences. Swim in one of the pools and turn the kids loose in the Dogpatch Playground. This is really the life—a vacation at Dogpatch U.S.A. right next door to the new Marble Falls Resort & Convention Center. There's always something to do the whole year 'round at these Great Twin Parks in the Ozarks.

TOP: Comedy skits were a recurring part of the live entertainment at the park. Here, town bully Earthquake McGoon makes his point forcefully during a "Dogpatch town council" routine. Other skits would erupt in the middle of the street, adding to the "anything can happen" flavor.

LEFT: When traditional thrill rides made their belated appearance at Dogpatch, there was at least some attempt to make them fit the theme. This one borrowed the aforementioned villain's name to become Earthquake McGoon's Brain Rattler.

TOP: The mystical, magical Shmoo became a nationwide fad after Al Capp introduced it into his comic strip in 1948. The smiling creature did not make it into the theme park until the 1980s, and one can only pity the employee who was elected to wear the "walking mattress" during the summer heat.

BOTTOM: After its park debut, the Shmoo took its place among the Dogpatch souvenirs, including these decals. As usual, the artwork was based on that of Al Capp without actually reproducing anything he had done.

For a summer 1985 Children's Festival, the usual cast of characters (in this case, McGoon and resident hag Nightmare Alice) were joined by Resource Raccoon, Heathcliff the comic strip cat, the Strawberry Shortcake gang and (not pictured) the Care Bears. If Al Capp had not died in 1979, it's easy to imagine the famously cynical cartoonist suffering severe nausea at the idea of such cutesy characters invading the Dogpatch world. *Doug Kirby/Roadside America.com collection.*

The traditional Capp characters, still in more or less recognizable form, pose on the park's swinging bridge for this late-era publicity shot. By that time, there were even locals who did not know the park was based on a long-discontinued comic strip and thought the characters had been created just to populate it.

OPPOSITE: Some reports claim that during Dogpatch's last couple of years in operation, it dropped the license from Al Capp's estate and existed without the comic strip tie-in. There is ample evidence that this was not strictly the case. For one, a dozen years after its final season, this informational sign still hung near the entrance, bringing visitors up to speed on what they were about to see.

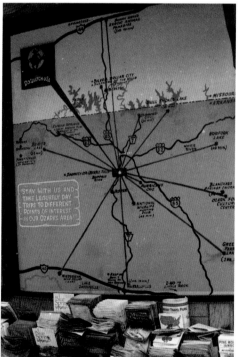

ABOVE: By 2005, this was all that remained of the signage directing tourists off State Highway 7 and into the Dogpatch parking lot. Four years after the park closed in 1993, the post office reverted to its original moniker of Marble Falls, Arkansas.

LEFT: Remarkably, another element that survived at the abandoned park's entrance was this map detailing the other Ozark attractions within driving distance. The brochures in the rack had likely not been replaced since the final 1993 operating season.

TOP: In 2005, the cars of the Dogpatch Decline ("or Incline, dependin' on which direction yo' is goin'," as the signs read) had been sitting idle for so long that trees and other underbrush had grown up inside them.

MIDDLE & BOTTOM: When the contents of the park were auctioned off to the highest bidder, these prime examples ended up with the owner of Lovejoy Collectibles in Harrison. They can still be enjoyed and admired by customers of that antiques store today.

By 2005, what was left of Dogpatch USA was a sad sight. This ruin was once the shop that sold honey, thus explaining the entrance resembling a giant honeycomb. The property has now been cleared of anything resembling its days as a comic strip theme park.

Three

THE SHOW MUST GO ON

Okay, we can hear what you are saying right about now. "How," you are gasping, with your eyes agog, "can the chapter on Ozark theater shows be the shortest one in the book, considering how much that industry has influenced Branson and its tourism?" Well, without knowing it, you have just answered your own question.

It is correct that dozens of live shows and theaters have thrived in Branson over the decades; so many, in fact, that to cover them comprehensively would take up the rest of the book. (Consult the bibliography to see how some other authors have approached the topic.) Also, remember that this book is about lost attractions, and there are shows still running that may be "lost" by the time it hits the shelves. For example, Branson's venerable Baldknobbers show began in 1959 and has been going so long that it should be bald and have knobby knees. But as of this writing, it is not a lost attraction.

Consider too that Branson is not the only focus of the book. As we shall see, there were small theaters and shows scattered throughout the northern Arkansas hills as well, but the second biggest concentration of them would have to be in the Lake of the Ozarks region. Lee Mace began his Ozark Opry show at Osage Beach in 1954, and it seemed it would never end. It did survive his 1985 death in a plane crash but finally saw its last performance in 2010. Ironically, the famous Ozark Opry building then became a Sears retail store. And as we all know, Sears stores are now lost attractions themselves.

So think of this chapter as a teeny-weeny overview of the theater side of the Ozarks. You won't see nearly all (or even most) of them but enough to give a general flavor of what used to keep audiences clapping and singing along far into the night.

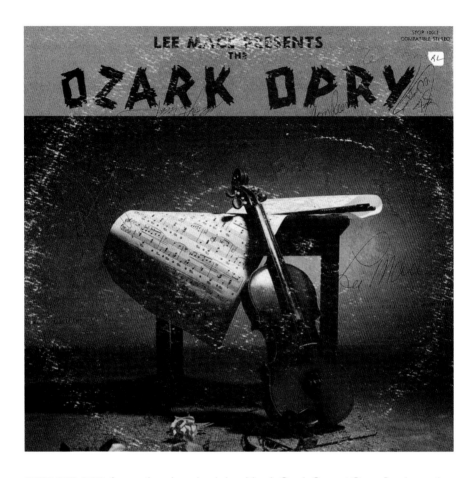

OPPOSITE, TOP: As mentioned previously, Lee Mace's Ozark Opry at Osage Beach was the forerunner of all the country music shows that would later thrive in both that area and in Branson. This theater building was constructed in 1957, and the neon sign became a landmark on the strip. *Todd Franklin collection.*

OPPOSITE, BOTTOM: The Ozark Opry benefited from having its performers highlighted on various Missouri TV stations during the off-season, when most attractions were closed. In this publicity photo, they are whooping it up on KRCG in Jefferson City, but the show was also carried via KMOS in Sedalia. When spring came, they would be right back at home in the Osage Beach theater.

ABOVE: Souvenir record albums were sold at the Ozark Opry, including this one. It may be difficult to see, due to the use of blue ballpoint ink, but this record jacket was autographed by most of the members of the cast, including resident comedian "Goofer" (Bill Atterberry).

4 Miles West of Branson, Missouri on Highway 76
Phone: (417) 334-0903

COUNTRY MUSIC COMEDY

ABOVE: Lee Mace died in a plane crash in 1985, but his wife maintained the Ozark Opry schedule until 2010. Afterward, the former theater building was gutted and turned into a Sears retail store, with a section devoted to displaying the Mace family's memorabilia. Now that Sears stores are as extinct as the Ozark Opry, the building was sitting empty again in 2022, although what was left of the original neon sign still pointed the way to the vacant edifice.

LEFT: Music shows in Branson began with the Mabe family's Baldknobbers Jamboree, which continues to this day. In the 1970s, Bob Mabe struck out on his own to begin the Bob-O-Link's Country Hoe-Down show, which continued the tradition of authentic hill country music.

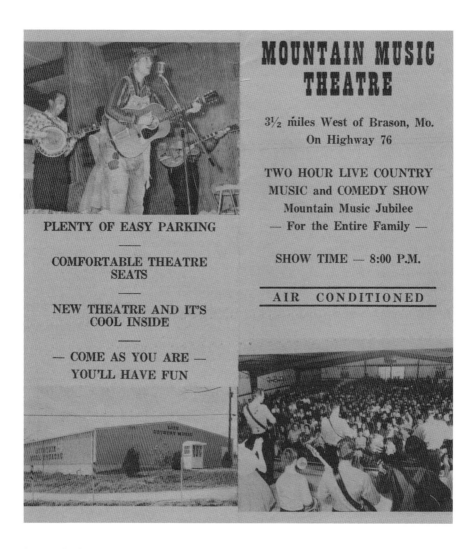

Branson's Mountain Music Theatre raised its curtain in 1967. It can be considered a lost attraction only because it no longer operates under that name. Visitors to Branson today can still enjoy its lineage under the current (and more well-known) name Presleys' Country Jubilee.

OPPOSITE: The 1980s were when the original family-owned shows in Branson began to be overshadowed—if not replaced completely—by an influx of big-money Las Vegas–type entertainment productions starring entertainers famous and not so famous. Pages and pages could be filled with brochures and advertisements for these seemingly countless shows, but due to space limitations—and the fact that this is not a book documenting Branson theater history—these four brochures will have to serve as a sampling.

ABOVE: Fortunately, we do not have to try to catalog all the Branson theaters in order to get an overview of them. Photographer Leland Payton captured these two incredible nighttime panoramas around 1991, when the Branson strip was at its peak of celebrity shows. You will no doubt be able to pick out the theaters belonging to John Davidson, Boxcar Willie and Roy Clark, but countless others are mixed in with them as well. *Crystal and Leland Payton collection; photos by Leland Payton.*

Not all Branson theaters relied on celebrity name recognition. Waltzing Waters was part of a tourism chain with locations in many different states, most famously in Florida. The name told it like it was: audiences sat in the darkened theater and watched sprays of water dance from hidden fountains, illuminated by colored floodlights and synchronized with recorded music. Some Waltzing Waters locations survive, but the one in Branson sprayed its last in 2013.

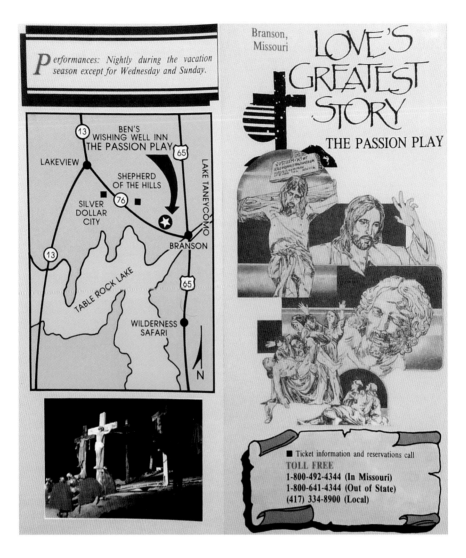

The most famous Passion Play in the Ozarks, of course, is the one in Eureka Springs, which began in 1968 and apparently will have eternal life. Not to be outdone, Branson attempted its own Passion Play for a short time, just down the street from the Shepherd of the Hills Farm. *Mark Pedro collection.*

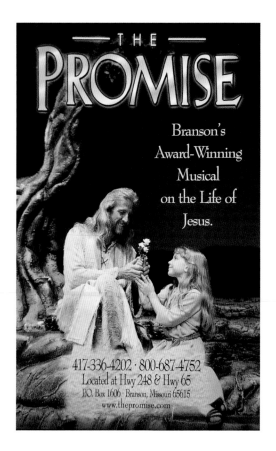

There was an offshoot of sorts from the traditional Passion Plays, in the form of these productions using huge casts and theatrical special effects to portray the life of Christ and other Bible-based themes. This one could be seen in Branson in 2001, but very similar productions turned up in tourist areas elsewhere, most notably in Pigeon Forge, Tennessee. *Mark Pedro collection.*

OPPOSITE, TOP: We must not forget that Ozark country music theaters actually began at Lake of the Ozarks and not Branson, and so we come to the Country Shindig Theatre, founded by Denny Hilton in 1969. It appears to have been a kissin' cousin to Lee Mace's Ozark Opry, even spurring a group of record albums featuring its cast. *Todd Franklin collection.*

OPPOSITE, BOTTOM: In Eureka Springs, the Pine Mountain Jamboree enjoyed a long run before closing for good in November 2015. This impressive brochure spread dates from its 1980 season, at which time things were still going strong.

Radio performer Louis Marshall Jones began calling himself "Grandpa" Jones while still in his twenties, because listeners thought his natural voice sounded like that of an old man. After gaining fame on the *Grand Ole Opry* and *Hee Haw*, Jones opened this dinner theater near his home in Mountain View in 1980. It lasted for a dozen years or so, and Jones continued wailing the daylights out of his banjo there whenever he was not on the road.

The combination of food and country music turned out to be a winning one in several different venues. In Hardy, the Arkansaw Traveller Folk Theatre began dishing up tunes and turnip greens in 1968.

★ ★ ★ ★ ★ ★ ★ ★ ★ ★ ★ ★

Frontier
Musicland Theatre
presents

Clean Family Entertainment
COUNTRY — COMEDY — GOSPEL
"Come as you are!"
Monday thru Saturday
April to November

Showtime 8 p.m.   Highway 178
501-445-4000   CITY OF
BULL SHOALS, ARKANSAS

TOP: Little information survives on the Frontier Musicland Theatre in Bull Shoals. It is notable that the logo character in this ad looks more like an off-model Yosemite Sam than a hillbilly. Maybe that's where the "frontier" part of the name originated. Its emphasis on "clean family entertainment" seems a bit unnecessary, since virtually all of these venues went out of their way to be inoffensive, usually incorporating gospel and patriotic songs among the hillbilly hijinks.

BOTTOM: Earlier we saw how the Ozark Opry cast members were TV regulars during the off-season. Perhaps the most beloved TV personality of the Ozarks was "Aunt Norma" Champion of KYTV in Springfield. From 1957 to 1986, in company with her puppet pals Rusty the Rooster and Skinny McGinnis, Champion entertained kids lucky enough to be in the TV station's broadcast range. Other local kids' TV hosts in the Ozarks included Ranger Ed and Timothy Beep in Joplin and Uncle Elmer in Fort Smith.

THE OZARKS

rolls out a red-carpet welcome for you, at

Silver Dollar City, Missouri

"Where the 1880 way of life lives on"

Near Branson and Springfield, Mo.

ON 2,000-ACRE MARVEL CAVE PARK

Performer Shad Heller served as the longtime blacksmith and unofficial mayor of Silver Dollar City. He played a major role in the episodes of *The Beverly Hillbillies* that were filmed at the park, and even returned to make additional appearances in the series afterward.

Four

AMUSEMENT PARK LARKS

This chapter and the next might be considered two parts of the same subject. For our purposes—which might not be everyone else's purposes—amusement parks have some combination of rides and/or games of skill (for example, miniature golf), whereas roadside attractions (discussed in chapter five) could range from wax museums to live animal exhibits and beyond. Dogpatch USA, which we have already visited, was a special case and thus deserved its own chapter, separate from the discussion of other amusement parks.

Whereas live shows and theaters were, and still are, thick around Branson, amusement parks did not truly catch on except for the legendary Silver Dollar City. Perhaps its drawing power is what prevented similar parks from trying to strike it rich. For whatever reason, most of the true amusement parks in this chapter grew up in the Lake of the Ozarks region.

There may be one reason for this, not immediately apparent. Lake of the Ozarks strove mightily to capture the aura of a beach resort, far from any salt water. Although the hillbilly theme gave it its own flavor (and that flavor wasn't saltwater taffy), many of the amusements and other attractions along the winding lake seem to have been inspired by those of the Atlantic and Gulf Coasts. And of course, no coastal resort would have been complete without an amusement park and goofy miniature golf courses.

That said, it must be admitted that the Ozarks amusement parks did not quite fit the "carnival" style so often encountered at seaside resorts. Even when they featured the same types of rides, they were couched in themes that would have seemed quite foreign to tourists in, say, Daytona Beach or Panama City Beach. Let's have a big meal of corn dogs and cotton candy and then get on a wildly spinning ride—we'll soon find out why they call it "fast food."

OPPOSITE: Many of the earliest amusement parks were begun by streetcar companies as a way to increase their own traffic. Joplin's Schifferdecker Electric Park was one of these. Like scores of amusement parks to come, it contained a ninety-six-foot-tall observation tower that gave an unequaled view of the surrounding countryside in those days when few people had ever gotten their feet off the ground.

ABOVE: It would be many years before the concept of a theme park jelled, but Joplin had a primitive version of one adjacent to the Junge Bakery. This 1931 view shows the giant Ozark mural that served as a backdrop to the landscaped trails with a miniature windmill and other sights. The park was dismantled during World War II.

One of Junge Park's most promoted features was its "animated electric sign" that changed scenes periodically. These two postcards are both dated 1940, which would have been shortly before the park was discontinued. One version shows the Easter scene, while the other features the characters from Walt Disney's *Snow White and the Seven Dwarfs*—thereby predating a more famous theme park in Anaheim, California, fifteen years in the future.

Silver Dollar City is today's most famous theme park in the Ozarks, but it didn't start out that way. In 1960, it was a collection of stores and other businesses on the site of a long-gone community called Marmaros, at the entrance to Marvel Cave near Branson. For a while it looked like Silver Dollar City was going to be yet another in a long line of Western theme parks, but it finally settled into recreating Ozark mountain life and then evolved into the conglomeration of rides that draws tourists away from Branson's live shows.

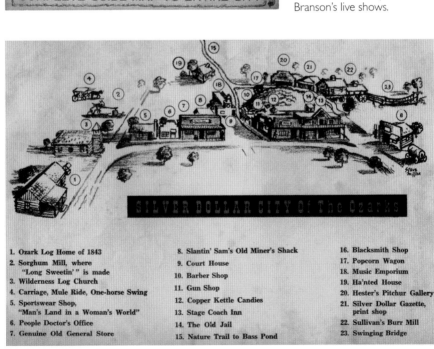

1. Ozark Log Home of 1843
2. Sorghum Mill, where "Long Sweetin'" is made
3. Wilderness Log Church
4. Carriage, Mule Ride, One-horse Swing
5. Sportswear Shop, "Man's Land in a Woman's World"
6. People Doctor's Office
7. Genuine Old General Store

8. Slantin' Sam's Old Miner's Shack
9. Court House
10. Barber Shop
11. Gun Shop
12. Copper Kettle Candies
13. Stage Coach Inn
14. The Old Jail
15. Nature Trail to Bass Pond

16. Blacksmith Shop
17. Popcorn Wagon
18. Music Emporium
19. Ha'nted House
20. Hester's Pitchur Gallery
21. Silver Dollar Gazette, print shop
22. Sullivan's Burr Mill
23. Swinging Bridge

OPPOSITE, TOP: Meanwhile, back at Osage Beach, Chet's Fun Spot was an "almost amusement park," but with lower-tech rides. It began as a restaurant and gift shop in 1954 before beginning to add other diversions during the next decade. Like most such enterprises, it was gone by the 1980s. *Todd Franklin collection.*

OPPOSITE, BOTTOM: Now, this was what most of us think of as a traditional amusement park. It must be admitted that the artist's depiction of a Wild Mouse ride does look more like Mad Mickey, however. *Todd Franklin collection.*

ABOVE: Most resort areas in the late 1960s and early 1970s had at least one of these giant slides, and Osage Beach was no exception. It might not be easy to see, but the participants sat on thick burlap sacks to keep their buns from burning on the hot metal slide. *Starr Johnson collection.*

Two Bit Town of Lake Ozark was yet another attraction that went after the hillbilly theme without totally immersing itself in it. The collection of rides and other entertainment operated from the late 1960s to sometime around 2015; parts of it continued in business after other sections were abandoned. *Todd Franklin collection.*

OPPOSITE: As much as anything else, Two Bit Town was known for its collection of fiberglass animals and mannequins, which were placed in deliberately surreal locations. Why else would there have been a polar bear on the roof of the Haunted Hotel, or even weirder, a hippopotamus head atop the fondly remembered Crazy Cousin's Cabin fun house? In Two Bit Town, none of it was supposed to make sense. *All, Todd Franklin collection.*

OPPOSITE, TOP: Two Bit Town also had a miniature-golf course as part of its entertainment complex. Although the sign was repainted more than once, it always featured some variation of this bent-over lady in short shorts that might have made Daisy Duke blush. (Daisy was from a different rural part of the country.) *Todd Franklin collection.*

OPPOSITE, BOTTOM: The Two Bit mini-golf was already gasping its last when photographer Debra Jane Seltzer made this photo in 2010. Most of the obstacles visible in this angle were manufactured by the Wittek Company of Chicago, which outfitted miniature-golf courses for decades. It is still in business but no longer deals in fiberglass animals and rotating windmills. *Debra Jane Seltzer collection.*

ABOVE: The nearest thing to the "coastal" style of miniature golf was Osage Beach's Goofy Golf, seen in our frontispiece. Giant concrete obstacles were the hallmark of Goofy Golf courses nationwide. One big difference is that the course in Osage Beach did not rely on dinosaurs to liven up the game. *Todd Franklin collection.*

LEFT, TOP & BOTTOM: The Ozarks' Goofy Golf made up for its lack of dinosaurs by sticking to its hillbilly theme as much as possible. The chicken house, where a hen would "lay" the golf ball, was a feature of other Goofy Golfs in faraway climes, whereas the penned pig and the hillbilly shack in the background were more localized citizens.

OPPOSITE, TOP: The turtle also had counterparts at other Goofy Golf courses, but each figure was custom-made out of concrete and chicken wire, so no two renditions could ever be exactly alike. *Todd Franklin collection.*

OPPOSITE, BOTTOM: The Jolly Golf courses were owned by the Sidwell family of Tennessee, and at their Osage Beach location they took up the prehistoric beasts flag that Goofy Golf had dropped. In fact, Jolly Golf's advertising promoted its status as "Land of the Dinosaurs." *Todd Franklin collection; photo by Neva Maddy.*

Another mini-golf chain that could be found on the Gulf Coast and in western states as well was Magic Carpet Golf. It came to the Lake of the Ozarks area but quickly disappeared as if by, well, magic.

OPPOSITE, TOP: After its too-brief career, Magic Carpet Golf saw its statuary and obstacles scattered among other courses in the area. This giant fish, seen in the previous photo, and a huge pirate ship were not so fortunate; as of this writing the pair sits on a back road far from the ballyhoo of the Lake of the Ozarks strip. The fish still has bright green Astroturf inside its mouth.

OPPOSITE, BOTTOM: Leaving Lake of the Ozarks temporarily, we find ourselves in Joplin again, where the mini-golf at Carousel Park closed in 2015. Until then, it had some charming hand-made figures, including this frog and alligator. *Debra Jane Seltzer collection.*

OPPOSITE: Branson has had, and still has, several entertainment complexes known simply as The Track. All have miniature golf in some form or another, but The Track location that boasted this Storybook Land course has now jumped the track and sent the nursery rhyme characters back to Mother Goose. *Both, Debra Jane Seltzer collection.*

ABOVE: Not all miniature-golf courses feature spectacular obstacles. This one near Bella Vista, Arkansas, photographed in the late 1980s, shows just how basic and unadorned such a facility can be when not trying to compete with other amusements. *Donnie Pitchford collection.*

ABOVE: The historical Fort Osage was nowhere near what would later become the Lake of the Ozarks region, instead situated near Kansas City. Still, an amusement park known as Fort of the Osage opened in Osage Beach around 1977 and attracted attention with this eye-catching entrance building. *Todd Franklin collection.*

OPPOSITE, TOP & MIDDLE: Fort of the Osage held down its fort for approximately a decade before the land was converted into other uses. Today, a highway runs through the middle of where the park used to be. The only visible remnant is the observation tower seen in this ad and souvenir pennant. The tower hoisted visitors aloft for a view of the surrounding area. Now inoperable, it still stands as a mute reminder of a long-gone fun spot. *Both, Todd Franklin collection.*

OPPOSITE, BOTTOM: With so much water at its disposal, the Lake of the Ozarks area quite naturally gravitated toward that old favorite, the water ski show. There was more than one of them in the area, but this happens to be the example that was part of the Fort of the Osage complex. *Todd Franklin collection.*

TOP: There was once a craze for Western-styled theme parks from coast to coast, tied mostly to the popularity of Western TV programs. Osage Beach was a bit late to the watering hole, with its Gold Nugget Junction not a-ridin' into town until 1972, by which time the only Western left on TV was the venerable *Gunsmoke*. *Todd Franklin collection.*

BOTTOM: Whether in California, New York, North Carolina or Florida (or any of two dozen other states), every Western park had to have a train ride. Gold Nugget Junction was no different, with this locomotive constantly circling the property.

Two other Gold Nugget Junction features that would have looked familiar to anyone who visited Knott's Berry Farm or Six Gun Territory or the others were the marshal shooting it out with the outlaws in the street and the saloon with its lovely ladies dancing on the stage. Of course, the gunfights were fake, but the women were certainly real. *Todd Franklin collection; Tim Williams collection.*

Lake of the Ozarks' NEW, Million-Dollar Family Fun Park!

family entertainment parks

Location: **Fun City USA** is located on the strip at Lake Ozark, Mo., near Bagnell Dam, on State Highway 54.

Hours: Open seven-days-a-week 10:00 a.m. to 1:00 a.m.

Family and Small Group plans available. *Large group* discount plans available in advance only. Write or call:

Sales Director, **Fun City USA**
Hwy. 54-B
Lake Ozark, Mo. 65049
(314) 365-2397

Member Bagnell Dam Chamber of Commerce

A Subsidiary of: UNITED ENTERTAINMENT GROUP, INC.

OPPOSITE, TOP: Somehow, pink does not seem to be the color one most readily thinks of when considering the Wild West, but it was Gold Nugget Junction's choice, and they stuck with it. The park holstered its six-guns and moseyed out of town in 1981. As of this writing, its former site remains a forested empty lot, quite unusual along the otherwise busy US 54 strip. *Todd Franklin collection.*

OPPOSITE, BOTTOM: The company that operated the Fun City USA amusement parks hedged its bet when it came to locations. As this brochure indicates, it had one park at Lake of the Ozarks and another at Rockaway Beach, part of Branson. It is not recorded what the Disney company thought about Fun City's appropriation of the Dumbo ride. *Todd Franklin collection.*

ABOVE: Ever heard the saying "Don't believe everything you read, Buster"? That applies to the Big Shot Amusement Park's signage denoting it as the "Lake's Premiere Family Attraction." The sign still stands over the decaying remains of the Big Shot facility in Linn Creek, two decades after the park's brief run ended in 2003.

Roadside attractions could range from extravaganzas costing millions to others for which a buck and a quarter might have been extreme. In the latter category was Eureka Springs' "Sliding Rock," where brides and grooms traditionally took the plunge for good luck. Here, it appears Mammy Yokum left Pappy back in Dogpatch to try to improve her own luck.

Five

FUN ALONG THE ROAD

While the chapter on theaters and shows is the shortest in this retrospective, we now come to the longest chapter. The reason should be abundantly clear: when it comes to roadside attractions, there is so much variety to be covered that even a multitude of photos can give only a brief overview of what once existed along Missouri and Arkansas highways.

As with the amusement parks in chapter four, the roadside attractions of the Ozarks frequently reflected what was going on in the rest of the country. Practically any attraction that could be found elsewhere also popped up in the Ozark country. Even so, there were certain localized themes, such as the previously examined abundance of hillbillies, that set the Ozark attractions apart from their kinfolk in other states.

One of the strangest was the seeming obsession Missouri attraction owners had with that ornery owlhoot outlaw Jesse James. Even if we ignore the fact that it would have been very difficult for Jesse to have traveled to as many different spots as traded on his legacy, we are still faced with his apparent lack of altruism. So the reasons for treating him as some sort of hero are best left for psychologists to explain.

But Jesse was not the only anomaly along the highways of the Ozarks. There were plenty of others, and they were scattered throughout the region. Naturally, big globs of them were concentrated in tourist centers such as Branson, Lake of the Ozarks and Eureka Springs, but they could easily be found anywhere in between as well. Better buckle your seat belts. This is going to be one wild ride.

Observation Tower and Hobby Shop
On U. S. 54, Lake of the Ozarks, Missouri

As briefly mentioned at the beginning of the previous chapter, one sure way of getting tourists to stop in the early days was to offer an observation tower of some sort. These two late 1930s postcards represent opposite sides of the state line. At both Lake of the Ozarks in Missouri and Mount Gayler in Arkansas, different approaches to the tower concept were built, but both had an accompanying gift shop and/or restaurant to go along with their free view of the scenery.

TOP: An early Ozarks resort was called Monte Ne, near Rogers, Arkansas. In 1925, construction began on what was intended to be a towering pyramid as a primary feature of the resort. Although funds ran out and construction ceased around 1936, the unfinished pyramid continued to be pictured on postcards for some years afterward.

BOTTOM: Roadside stands such as this one satisfied tourists' desires for authentic Ozark crafts, food and drink. And yes, it too had a "free scenic tower," although this one does not look like it would provide much of a view. It was near Branson at Chula Vista.

Not all gift shops were as authentic as others. The Tepee Gift Shop at Mountainburg, Arkansas, employed Plains Indians imagery, several thousand miles from those tribes' home turf. Still, running across a shop like this was a welcome respite during a long day's auto trip. *John Margolies collection.*

OPPOSITE: With such a vast expanse of water, naturally Lake of the Ozarks was a logical choice for excursion boats, several of which could be found operating at any given time. These two views are of the *Larry Don*, one of the most popular, whether in its original two-deck or later triple-deck configuration. The *Larry Don* sank in the drink in 2014 and was later scrapped. *Bottom, Todd Franklin collection.*

The "Larry-Don" Excursion Boat, Lake of the Ozarks, Missouri

LEFT: Now we come to a whole herd of animal attractions of various stripes. Exotic Animal Paradise near Springfield was part of a subset that allowed the visitors to drive through simulated habitats and view the beasts roaming freely. The idea saw its greatest use in the chain of Lion Country Safari parks in the 1970s.

OPPOSITE, TOP: Exotic Animal Paradise was built by former rancher Pat Jones in 1971. It closed in 2006, but not long thereafter it was reborn as part of the Wild Animal Safari chain, another close relation to Lion Country Safari. *John Margolies collection.*

OPPOSITE, BOTTOM: Osage Beach's African Lion Safari did not do much to hide its similarity to Lion Country Safari. Besides the obligatory drive-through, it also advertised such additional features as a Junior Jungle Petting Zoo, Parrot Island, elephant rides and Hessi Waterfalls, "where the fish eat out of your hands." *Todd Franklin collection.*

LOCATION: African Lion Safari is situated in the beautiful Lake of the Ozarks area at Osage Beach just off Route 54 at Y Road; follow the directional signs.

HOURS: 9:00 AM to 1 Hour before sundown, seven days a week.

PRICES: Adults, $2.00; Children five through fourteen, $1.50; four years and under, free.

GROUP RATES: On request.

PETS: No pets allowed.

JUST OFF ROUTE 54
ON Y ROAD
OSAGE BEACH, MISSOURI

A WILD ANIMAL PRESERVE DRIVE-THROUGH

HERE'S HOW TO GET TO

TOM'S MONKEY JUNGLE

Located on Highway 54 Near Eldon, Mo.
(Next to Corral Drive-In Theatre)

Souvenirs TO FIT EVERY PURPOSE

At Tom's Monkey Jungle you will find a large variety of beautiful and useful gifts and at prices surprisingly low. Our courteous attendants will gladly show you any gift in the place with no obligation to purchase. There are plenty of sensible gifts for the kiddies.

If you are honeymooners, be sure and get your free gift at the souvenir counter.

See the pets in our cool, shady jungle and buy your gifts in our air-conditioned gift shop.

YOU'RE NEVER TOO OLD FOR

TOM'S MONKEY JUNGLE

MANY UNUSUAL ANIMALS AND BIRDS

SEVERAL FOR YOU TO PET

This jungle is the result of a lifetime ambition to visit a zoo where there would be cute, clever and tame animals that children and adults alike would enjoy. A zoo where the animals could be held and petted. This is truly a new experience with birds and animals.

"U-Otter C R Otters" and have your picture taken with our tame Honey Bears or Monkeys. A special attraction for the kiddies is our Storybook Land.

YOU'RE NEVER TOO OLD FOR
TOM'S MONKEY JUNGLE

AND ALL FROM FOREIGN LANDS

"HEY"

KIDS

STORY

BOOK

LAND

2½ Acres of Shaded Garden

Located on Highway 54 Near Eldon, Mo.
(Next to Corral Drive-In Theatre
10½ Miles North of Bagnall Dam)

Relax With Us — Use
Our Free Picnic
Facilities

OPPOSITE: One genre of attraction missing from the Ozarks was the Santa Claus–themed park. But the Ozark Deer Farm at Eldon did its part to keep the idea alive, naming several of its deer Dancer, Prancer, Rudolph and so forth. Also on the premises was the heavily promoted five-legged ox. (The extra appendage protruded from its shoulder, not underneath with the rest of the legs.)

ABOVE: Tom's Monkey Jungle could be found in proximity to the Ozark Deer Farm, perhaps explaining why monkeys and deer could be found at both parks. Tom's had many other animals as well, many of the tropical variety, which makes one wonder how they got along in the decidedly non-tropical climate of the Ozarks. *Todd Franklin collection.*

These images show just how closely Tom's Monkey Jungle resembled its scores of cousins along the highways in the days when animal welfare was not as much of a concern. Tom's even went to the extreme of selling monkeys to tourists, which must have resulted in some interesting stories about the drive home—and what happened when the neighbors found out. *Both, Todd Franklin collection.*

LEFT: Eldon's Animal World was not one of the drive-through parks but instead was more like a zoo. It was yet another attraction that opened in the 1970s and closed in the 1990s, with no specific dates for either event apparently having been recorded. *Todd Franklin collection.*

BELOW: Some twenty years after its demise, the ruins of Animal World could still be seen in Eldon. This deteriorating monkey-bedecked sign was part of that, but within another couple of years all traces of the park had been cleared away. As of this writing, the only visible remnant is the former entrance gate. *Todd Franklin collection.*

MAX ALLEN'S ZOOLOGICAL GARDENS, Eldon, Mo., on U.S. 54

OPPOSITE, TOP: Almost adjacent to the Animal World property was Max Allen's Zoological Gardens, alternately (and better) known as Max Allen's Reptile Gardens. One might be tempted to think this attraction was related to Ross Allen's Reptile Institute in Florida, but there was apparently no connection. The owner was Max Allen Nickerson, of the Nickerson Farms restaurant family (about which more in our next chapter). *Todd Franklin collection.*

OPPOSITE, BOTTOM: In the spring of 2022, the rockwork walls of Max Allen's snake farm were still standing, but the rest of the building was in ruins. At one point some of its painted signs like this one were still visible, but the foliage has now obscured any that might have survived. *Todd Franklin collection.*

ABOVE: It was one thing to see and pet (and smell) live animals, but some tourists preferred seeing the ones that were already dead and stuffed. One such taxidermy display was the Call of the Wild Museum at Poplar Bluff, consisting of J.R. Baker's big-game hunting collection. In a strange twist, after the museum closed it was converted into an—ahem—"gentlemen's club" and retained its traditional rock façade while promoting a different type of call of the wild. *John Margolies collection.*

ROGERS

ANIMAL KINGDOM

(ON THE ROAD TO SILVER DOLLAR CITY)

HWY. 76
ONE MILE WEST OF
BRANSON, MO
OPEN 7 DAYS A WEEK — PH: 417-334-5258

LEFT: Down in Branson, formerly living creatures were also featured in their eternal state at Rogers' Animal Kingdom. As the full-body tiger on the front of the brochure indicates, some of the trophies were species that are now illegal to hunt.

OPPOSITE: We now transition from big-game animals to prehistoric ones and arrive in Beaver, Arkansas, to visit Dinosaur World. That must be Fred Flintstone's uncouth Neanderthal ancestor waiting to greet us at the ticket booth. *Both, John Margolies collection.*

OPPOSITE: When Dinosaur World opened in 1962, it was known as Farwell's Dinosaur Park. This early postcard likely dates from that period. It was a different tourism world then, when people dressed in their Sunday-go-to-meetin' clothes to visit concrete sauropods. *Debra Jane Seltzer collection.*

ABOVE: Anatomical and historical accuracy were not always the main focus at Dinosaur World, but with its one hundred statues situated along a two-mile trail, quantity was more important than quality. According to those in the know, the path could be covered on foot or by vehicle. *John Margolies collection.*

BEAR
The distinctive feature of this bear is the fact that the body contains a hive of bees. During the warm summer days the bees may be observed passing in and out of the open mouth.

FISHING LAKE

Other replicas in the park include Saber-Tooth Cat, Parasaurolophus, Trachodon, Ceratosaurus, Ankilausus, Fulvustincus, Buffulo, Pteranodon, Phytosaur, Brontops, Eohippus, Notharctus, Saltoposuchus, Lizard, Octopus, Cave Men, Glyptodont, Unitarium, and many others.

Noted sculptor and paleontologist Emmet Sullivan was commissioned by Ola Farwell to create these selections of full scale dinosaur models of the Paleozoic, Mesozoic and Cenozoic Eras. Sculptor Sullivan spent most of his life in the western United States, an area especially rich in fossil remains, and was attracted at an early age to the study of these fascinating creatures. His discoveries have contributed much to science.

Bumper Boats
LAND OF KONG

Experience the Thrills of
John Agar's
LAND OF KONG
Near Eureka Spring, Arkansas

(Kong Attending to the Villain)

65 ACRES LIFE-SIZE
DINOSAURS

FUN — FUN — FUN
BUMPER BOATS — PADDLE BOATS
FISHING LAKE — PLAYGROUND
CAFE — GIFT SHOP
CAMPGROUND — FULL HOOKUPS

After an ownership change in the early 1980s, the park became John Agar's Land of Kong, named after a busy actor who had appeared in dozens of sci-fi thrillers in the 1940s, 1950s and 1960s. At the entrance, a giant replica of the title ape (Kong, not Agar) waved menacingly. It was not enough to keep things going, and the re-renamed Dinosaur World closed in 2005. *Top, Doug Kirby/RoadsideAmerica.com collection; bottom, John Margolies collection.*

Northwestern Arkansas might seem an odd place to find numerous statues of that one-eyed seafarer Popeye the Sailor, but it was in Alma that a Popeye brand of spinach was first canned in 1965. With several canneries churning out the strength-giving product, eventually some unique Popeye statues sprouted in their neighborhoods. Some still exist, but this one in Siloam Springs has sailed away into the sunset. Without a pipe, he wasn't even able to "toot toot" as he did so. *Donnie Pitchford collection.*

Jesse James Museum & Confusion Hill

½ Mile West on Highway 76
BRANSON, MISSOURI

Phone ED 4-3594

OPPOSITE: Earlier, we mentioned Missouri tourism's seeming obsession with Jesse James. There is no documentation that he ever attended one of the music shows in Branson, but the town did have a mini-Jesse theme park of sorts. This rearing fiberglass horse served as the roadside lure.

LEFT & BELOW: Besides the (one of several in the state) Jesse James Wax Museum, the Branson complex featured Confusion Hill, one of the innumerable "gravity" attractions that could be found in, and in between, practically any resort area. Its connection to Jesse James's masked mug was tenuous at best.

JESSE JAMES MUSEUM — CONFUSION HILL
½ Mile West on Highway 76, Branson, Missouri

Wax figures of
famous outlaws

⬅

· · · · · And people, Too!

103

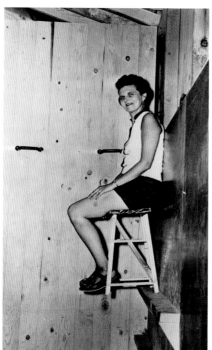

Balancing Stool at Phantom Acres
Bagnell Dam, Mo.

Naturally, the laws of gravity went bonkers up at Lake of the Ozarks as well, with the Phantom Acres tilted house causing visitors to stand at odd angles and chairs to stick to the wall. At least they didn't try to blame Jesse James for the weird goings-on. *Both, Todd Franklin collection.*

But oh, no, Lake of the Ozarks wasn't about to be left out of the Jesse sweepstakes. This unusual postcard was printed with the same info and graphics going in both directions so that it could not be viewed upside-down. The back of the postcard makes reference to "handsome Jesse James," although in real life few people could have ever seen his unmasked face and lived to brag about it. *Both, Todd Franklin collection.*

OPPOSITE, TOP: Branson has had its share of non-Jesse wax museums over the years, and the tradition continues to this day. Here is one that did not survive, although as with most defunct wax museums, its semi-reasonable facsimiles of living and dead celebrities have probably been repurposed in other facilities across the country. *Mark Pedro collection.*

OPPOSITE, BOTTOM: Western good guy Roy Rogers established his own museum in Victorville, California, in 1976. After the death of his wife, "Queen of the West" Dale Evans, the museum moved to Branson in 2003. But its lifespan there was brief. It closed in 2009, and the artifacts—including the taxidermied remains of Trigger the horse and Bullet the dog—were auctioned off to collectors the following year. *Doug Kirby / RoadsideAmerica.com collection.*

ABOVE: In 2010, this toy museum inside a former Stuckey's along Route 66 in Stanton was going out of business and liquidating its collection of vintage items. Directly next door was—wait for it—another Jesse James Museum. It escaped inclusion in this book because, as of this writing, it is still in business.

TOP: Most roadside attractions do whatever is necessary to make themselves stand out from their surroundings. The Miles Mountain Musical Museum in Eureka Springs seems to have taken the opposite approach. One could have been forgiven for thinking it was an abandoned apartment house or dormitory.

BOTTOM: The Miles Mountain Musical Museum's souvenirs were far more attractive than its building. This small collection of them can be seen in a museum in Branson. The music museum itself advertised that its musical instruments were augmented by paintings, clocks, woodcarvings and a fluorescent rock display. A Dairy D'sert snack bar stood nearby.

TOP: Another huge part of Ozarks tourism was the many caves that existed underneath the mountains. Some of them are now classified as lost attractions, even though technically the caves are still there—just not open to the public. Truitt's Cave near Lanagan, Missouri, opened around 1940, but just when its commercial tours ceased is less certain. Its associated dining room continues to operate today.

BOTTOM: Another cave that combined dining with spelunking was Wonder Cave near Bella Vista, Arkansas. This postcard dates from the days when it was enjoying a career as a nightclub, complete with dance floor and bandstand. It has been alternately known as Wonderland Cave, with signage depicting Alice and her underground companions. So far, attempts to restore and reopen it seem to have fallen down a rabbit hole.

Adoration Scene Atop Mt. Branson, Branson, Missouri

OPPOSITE: Missouri's most famous cave, of course, is Meramec Caverns ("Jesse James' Hideout," for those who are keeping track of ol' Jesse). It is still a major attraction along Route 66, but less common are the painted barns that once blanketed the roadside, advertising the attraction. Owner Lester Dill is said to have received his inspiration from seeing painted barn roofs in Tennessee, and his use of white letters on a black background would indicate that it was the legendary "See Rock City" barns that gave him the idea. As seen here, the barn signs later became a little more colorful. *Both, Russell Wells collection.*

ABOVE: In 1949, Branson began the tradition of erecting an enormous Nativity scene atop a nearby mountain during the Christmas season. The largest figure was twenty-four feet tall, and when illuminated at night, the tableau could be seen from four miles away. The original scene depicted in this postcard is now a lost attraction, as is anything resembling this Branson streetscape. But a new display was crafted in 2012 to revive the custom.

Charles Dickens Land of Enchantment

★ A Family Excursion Thru Christmas Past, Future And Present.

★ Over 200 Life-Size Automated Animated Characters In 50 Disneyland-Like Displays.

"The Story of Scrooge"
Life-size animated caricatures
in realistic displays.

Story "Birth of Christ"
in life-like setting
with live animals.

★ Inspirational Traditional Stories Of Christmas.

★ Birth of Christ, Scrooge, Santa Claus, Rudolph Red-Nosed Reindeer, Live Animals, Etc.

"Fairy Tales of Christmas"
From Rudolph the Red-Nosed Reindeer to
Charlie Brown in life-size displays.

Fun For Kids 2 To 92

"Santa Claus' North Pole Home"
Tons of snow, trees. It's so real!

ABOVE: Speaking of Christmas, that was the year-round theme of a short-lived Eureka Springs attraction known as Charles Dickens' Land of Enchantment. In a non-air-conditioned building, animated figures in snowy landscapes acted out highlights from *A Christmas Carol* and from more modern tales such as *A Charlie Brown Christmas* and *Rudolph the Red-Nosed Reindeer*. This brochure has the only known photos of these scenes, which show that any resemblance between them and their source material was strictly accidental. *Doug Kirby / RoadsideAmerica.com collection.*

OPPOSITE: We have already seen examples of Ozark attractions that were inspired by their cousins in Florida, but this one had a genuine Sunshine State lineage. The Aquarama at Osage Beach was admittedly influenced by Florida's Weeki Wachee Spring and its underwater theater with performing mermaids. In fact, some of the ladies from Weeki Wachee traveled to Lake of the Ozarks to help train their hill country counterparts for its 1964 opening. The Aquarama stayed afloat until 1973. *Both, Todd Franklin collection.*

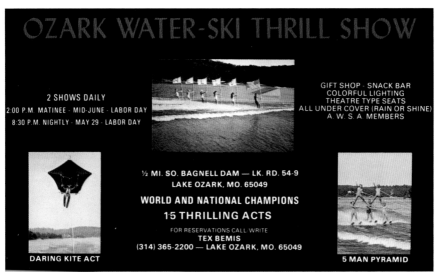

OPPOSITE, TOP: In the previous chapter we saw the water ski show at Fort of the Osage amusement park, but here is an even better example of that genre of attraction. The "Thrill Show" had elements that certainly had kinship at Florida's Cypress Gardens, but many of the same stunts were simultaneously being performed in the less subtropical atmosphere of the Wisconsin Dells. *Todd Franklin collection.*

OPPOSITE, BOTTOM: In chapter two, remember that rack of brochures left to the elements after Dogpatch USA closed in 1993? This spread comes from one of those, advertising the Ramada Inn of Harrison, Arkansas. No, a motel could not technically qualify as an attraction, but those shots of the pool and the video arcade certainly represent their era, when such motel chains attempted to provide as much entertainment as possible for their guests' antsy children.

ABOVE: Finally, we come to a more recent attraction that had a very brief life. The Ozark Medieval Fortress near Lead Hill, Arkansas, was reminiscent of that 1920s attempt to build a pyramid at Monte Ne—and was just about as successful. The idea was to build a replica of a French castle (thirteenth-century vintage) by using only materials and construction techniques of that time. A natural fit for the Ozarks, wouldn't you say? *Janet McMurrin collection.*

For the one year or so the Ozark Medieval Fortress operated, reenactors in period costume demonstrated the thirteenth-century way of doing things. The weaving display furnished its own raw materials thanks to the woolly sheep in an adjacent pen. The projected revenue never magically materialized, and at last report the unfinished fortress still sat abandoned. At least someone didn't raze it to build a Walmart on the spot. *Both, Janet McMurrin collection.*

Six

READING THE SIGNS

We now come to our grand finale, the "catchall" chapter that gathers whatever we might have managed to miss in the previous five. The simplest way to do that is to take a tour through the most spectacular signage that lined the highways in those long-ago days. And as far as we know, the signs chosen for this chapter either no longer exist, or the businesses they promoted are now defunct.

Many people have probably never stopped to think about what a large role signage has played in their nostalgic memories. After a long day of driving, there was nothing more comforting than a brightly colored neon sign in front of a cozy motel. If that sign were gigantic, such as the neon spectaculars employed by Holiday Inn and Howard Johnson's, so much the better.

But in between those overnight stops there were many other types. There were billboards that gave kids and their weary parents something to read in the days before handheld screens. There were gas stations, which attempted to build brand loyalty when all gas was cheap and there was really no other way of distinguishing themselves. And of course there was the middle element of the "gas, food and lodging" triumvirate, as travelers could hardly be expected to keep going on empty stomachs. From sit-down restaurants to drive-up drive-ins, all used their signage to pull in those who were craving a meal.

So, as we drive off into the sunset (assuming we are traveling west—otherwise, never mind), let's look at some of that classic signage that helped make a road trip a little less monotonous. Although gone now, they deserve the same recognition as the attractions and amusements that were the main goal of any family vacation. Here we can revisit them one more time.

Many travelers along Route 66 were undoubtedly relieved to see this generic "MOTEL" sign at Pacific, Missouri, towering in the distance. Even with its letter *E* missing, it still has the power to evoke a bygone day of tourism. *Russell Wells collection.*

OPPOSITE: Also on Route 66 in Missouri, this time at Newburg, the ruins of John's Modern Cabins have become something of a pilgrimage for highway historians. Chief among the reasons is the now-ironic juxtaposition of the business name with such a pile of rubble. But that neon sign once beckoned to tired drivers just as heartily as any of the others. *Both, Russell Wells collection.*

OPPOSITE, TOP: Sometimes motel names simply defied logic. Let's take the Western Air Motel in Fort Smith. It would only seem "Western" to those from east of the Mississippi River, perhaps, but that saguaro cactus on its sign really seemed to be stretching the point. This is a good example of the tourism staple of making people feel they were somewhere else when they were already somewhere else.

OPPOSITE, BOTTOM: Incredibly, elsewhere in Fort Smith, the Stonewall Jackson Inn has survived, but not this neon masterpiece of a sign. Instead of leading his troops in a charge, doesn't it look more like ol' Stonewall is riding a merry-go-round horse? *John Margolies collection.*

ABOVE: In Osage Beach, the Golden Door Motel and its revolving door sign survived longer than many of its brethren in the hospitality field. Opening in 1964, the motel left the door open for tourists until 2017, when the property was sold for other purposes.

In 2015, this lonely sign was all that remained of the Town and Country Motel that once sat at an I-44 exit between Joplin and Springfield. An antiques mall at the same exit was also barely hanging on and has since faded into the same history as the collectibles it sold.

OPPOSITE, TOP: Early motels in the Best Western chain were still independent mom-and-pop operations, but they were authorized to display the Best Western signage as a mark of quality. The Alamo Motel in Walnut Ridge, Arkansas, was one such licensee. Note how elaborate the Best Western logo was in those days, with chasing lights making the crown sparkle at night. As for its Davy Crockett Restaurant, the king of the wild frontier must have stopped there during his journey from Tennessee to the Alamo.

OPPOSITE, BOTTOM: The TraveLodge chain distinguished itself with its "Sleepy Bear" mascot, groping his way across ads in silhouette and in full form on the signage. (But why is he aqua blue instead of his usual brown?) This one was in Newport, Arkansas, but Sleepy could be found sleepwalking on a path from coast to coast.

ABOVE: The Howard Johnson's Motor Lodges were so successful that they eventually came to replace the older namesake restaurants. This complex, from when both types of orange-roofed businesses were still part of the mix, stretched for quite some distance alongside US 54 at Lake Ozark. (In case you have not been keeping up on such things, the restaurants used Simple Simon and the Pieman as their logo, while the motor lodges kept Simon but replaced the pastry chef with the old lamplighter of long, long ago.)

OPPOSITE: In the previous chapter, we briefly glimpsed this Jesse James Motel sign at the masked man's attraction in Branson. Here is a more spectacular twilight view of its glowing neon. Note that photographer Leland Payton quite incidentally captured a second now-lost roadside sight on the other side of the highway: an outlet of the short-lived Kenny Rogers Roasters chicken chain. *Crystal and Leland Payton collection; photo by Leland Payton.*

THE FAMOUS

aq®

RUSSELLVILLE, ARKANSAS

CHICKEN HOUSE

HIGHWAY 64 EAST
ONLY ONE MINUTE OFF
INTERSTATE 40

PHONE 501-968-2100

serving the world's finest fried chicken

Speaking of chicken, the chain of AQ ("Arkansas Quality") Chicken Houses began in Springdale, Arkansas, in 1947. By the time of this 1970s ad, they had expanded across the Ozarks, including this one in Russellville. The chain has now contracted back to the original Springdale location, which maintains the same logo but not this sign with its giant drumstick. (As a side note, there actually was a chain called Ozark Fried Chicken, but it was based in Texas and apparently never had locations anywhere near its namesake mountains.)

OPPOSITE, TOP: The Diamonds Restaurant on Route 66 at Villa Ridge, Missouri, employed a bit of hyperbole in calling itself the largest such establishment in the country. Be that as it may, it was certainly a landmark in that part of the Ozarks. When the original structure burned in 1948, a gleaming new edifice rose in its place.

OPPOSITE, BOTTOM: In the late 1960s, the Diamonds moved to a new location, which has since closed. Other restaurants occupied the former 1948 Art Deco building, but as seen here in 2017, it too has become a forlorn reminder of what once was. *Russell Wells collection.*

THE DIAMONDS RESTAURANT AND CABINS

JUNCTION 50-66-100   VILLA RIDGE, MO.

ABOVE: Route 66 provided part of the logo for Springfield's Campbell 66 Express truck line. Its trailers bearing the image of Snortin' Norton the Camel ("Humpin' to Please") were once common sights on the nation's highways. They now only occasionally turn up abandoned in fields or junkyards.

LEFT: In Springdale, Arkansas, we've already heard from AQ's Chicken House, but Heinie's Steak House wasn't exactly dragging up the rear. It was the place to go for those craving more than just fried chicken, and with a neon chef's face on the sign, how could they go wrong? *John Margolies collection.*

OPPOSITE: This ad for the Pioneer Restaurant in Hardy, Arkansas, makes it appear to be a relative of the dinner theaters in Branson—although on a much, much smaller scale and lower budget.

PIONEER RESTAURANT

Excellent Food. Friendly Service. Live Entertainment.

Bring the entire family down to enjoy a delicious meal in our comfortable, rustic atmosphere. All meals are carefully prepared to give you the best in dining pleasure.

Enjoy live country and western music on Friday and Saturday nights, featuring The Dusty Rhodes Show with Rhodes, Chalmers and Rhodes as special guest stars.

No cover charge. Located at the east edge of Hardy at U.S. 62 and 63. Phone (501) 856-8196.

When John Margolies found this pristine marquee for the Grove Drive-In Theatre in Springdale, Arkansas, his photographer's eye must have been struck by the incongruity. Note the snow on the ground coupled with the image of neon palm trees on the sign. For that matter, any palm trees in the Arkansas Ozarks would have been pretty incongruous, even in the middle of the summer. *John Margolies collection.*

OPPOSITE, TOP: At the Lone Star Court—apparently named after its neon emblem and not the state of Texas—travelers on Route 66 could get their gas, food and lodging needs all in one place. Note the "torch and oval" Standard Oil sign, which later became the emblem for the American Oil stations, aka Amoco.

OPPOSITE, BOTTOM: The Derby Oil gas stations were primarily confined to the midwestern states. This one in St. James, Missouri, appears to have become old hat a long time ago. *Russell Wells collection.*

OPPOSITE: In Clarksville, Arkansas, this friendly giant was born as the emblem of the Texaco service stations, known in a 1960s ad campaign as the "Big Friend." His employment as "the man who wears the star / the big, bright Texaco star" was brief, and the various Big Friend statues nationwide ended up either junked or repainted to serve other purposes. *John Margolies collection.*

ABOVE: One might be tempted to think the community of Gascozark, Missouri, was named after a gas station. Actually, the name was a combination of the surrounding Ozarks and the nearby Gasconade River. But it was indeed coined by the owner of this café on Route 66, which sold gas both by the gallon and by the plate. *Russell Wells collection.*

The chain of Stuckey's stores was entrenched in the southeastern states, but franchisee I.J. Nickerson opened the first Stuckey's west of the Mississipi River at Eldon, Missouri. The story goes that Nickerson got crossways with W.S. Stuckey over wanting to have a true sit-down restaurant instead of Stuckey's traditional snack bar. Ultimately, Nickerson decided to strike out on his own. *Bob Cara collection.*

OPPOSITE, TOP: The answer to Stuckey's was Nickerson Farms, a chain that did have true restaurants instead of snack bars along with its selection of gifts and souvenirs. Based in Eldon from beginning to end, Nickerson Farms was extremely popular in the Midwest but eventually bought the farm—Nickerson, that is—and only a few repurposed buildings with their pointed red rooflines can be found today.

OPPOSITE, BOTTOM: Wow, talk about a shop that presented a bunch of mixed tourism messages all at once. Pecan Joe's could be found along Route 66 at Newburg, Missouri, although pecans were more usually found in shops such as Stuckey's in the Southeast. But even granting that, with its southwestern decor and a logo of a pecan wearing a sombrero, it looked like it belonged in southern Texas instead of in the Ozarks.

In contrast to Pecan Joe's, here is a gift shop that perfectly fit its location in the Lake of the Ozarks region. Buildings using that type of stonework as their surfacing (see the Gascozark Café a few pages back) could be found in practically any mountain tourist region. This one later became a much-loved pizza parlor adjacent to Bagnell Dam.

OPPOSITE: Remember how the Dogpatch complex in Osage Beach could not use the trademarked images of the Al Capp *Li'l Abner* characters? Elsewhere in Osage Beach, the Ozark Maid Candy Kitchen decided to risk Capp's wrath by making the figure on their sign look as much like Daisy Mae as possible. This ad dates from 1972, by which time the "real" Daisy Mae and her cohorts were cavorting at Dogpatch USA.

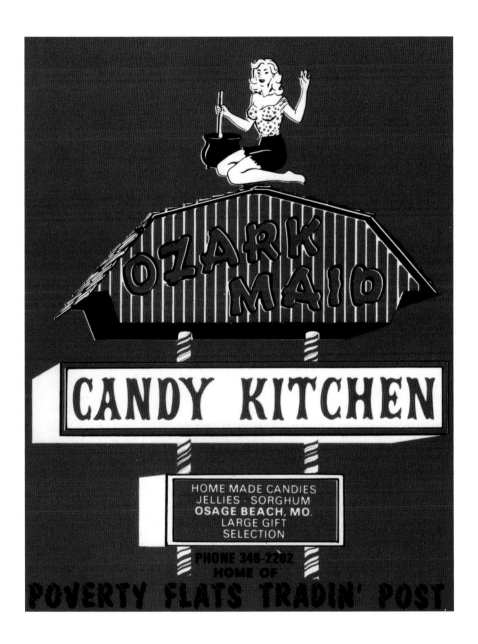

In a rather unusual turn of events, not only is the Barefoot Traders Gift Shop and its sign a lost attraction, so is the small Missouri town of Lakeside where it operated. Despite its location along US 54 and the busy Bagnell Dam strip, during the past twenty years, the population of Lakeside dropped from thirty-seven to zero. *John Margolies collection.*

OPPOSITE, TOP: The razorback hog has long been the emblem of the University of Arkansas. This gift shop was located in Mountain Home, quite some distance from the college campus in Fayetteville, but the snorting pigs could be found just about anywhere in the state. Note that cutout hillbilly figures were holding their own at this small store too. *John Margolies collection.*

OPPOSITE, BOTTOM: In Hardy, Arkansas, could be found the Frontier Curio Shop, selling a little of anything tourists might be willing to buy. Its advertising of antiques among the inventory is amusing with the hindsight that even its modern-day merchandise would be likely to turn up in any antiques mall or collectibles store today.

And we finally come down to this. The Skyvue neon sign in Salem, Arkansas, might not necessarily be classified as a lost attraction. Not yet, anyway. According to the website for the strip shopping center it promotes, the business is still a going concern. When visited in the spring of 2022, however, this sign was holding a lonely vigil over what appeared to be an empty set of buildings. Hopefully the Skyvue and its sign will manage to hang in there until better days instead of joining its companions in the rest of this book.

BIBLIOGRAPHY

Baeder, John. *Gas, Food and Lodging*. New York: Abbeville Press, 1982.

Blevins, Brooks. *Arkansas/Arkansaw: How Bear Hunters, Hillbillies and Good Ol' Boys Defined a State*. Fayetteville: University of Arkansas Press, 2009.

Geist, Bill. *Lake of the Ozarks*. New York: Grand Central Publishing, 2019.

Harkins, Anthony. *Hillbilly: A Cultural History of an American Icon*. New York: Oxford University Press, 2004.

Hollis, Tim. *Ain't That a Knee Slapper: Rural Comedy in the 20ᵗʰ Century*. Jackson: University Press of Mississippi, 2008.

———. *Dixie Before Disney: 100 Years of Roadside Fun*. Jackson: University Press of Mississippi, 1999.

———. *Toons in Toyland: The Story of Cartoon Character Merchandise*. Jackson: University Press of Mississippi, 2015.

Margolies, John. *Miniature Golf*. New York: Abbeville Press, 1987.

Payton, Leland, and Crystal Payton. *Branson: Country Themes and Neon Dreams*. Branson, MO: Anderson Publishing, 1993.

———. *See the Ozarks: The Touristic Image*. Springfield, MO: Lens and Pen Press, 2003.

———. *The Story of Silver Dollar City*. Springfield, MO: Lens and Pen Press, 1997.

Roberts, Anita L. *Images of America: Branson*. Charleston, SC: Arcadia Publishing, 2014.

Wallis, Michael. *Route 66: The Mother Road*. New York: St. Martin's Press, 1990.

Weaver, H. Dwight. *Images of America: Lake of the Ozarks, Vintage Vacation Paradise*. Charleston, SC: Arcadia Publishing, 2002.

———. *Images of America: Osage Beach*. Charleston, SC: Arcadia Publishing, 2012.

ABOUT THE AUTHOR

Tim Hollis has written thirty-seven books on pop culture history, a number of them concerning southeastern tourism. He also operates his own museum of vintage toys, souvenirs and other pop culture artifacts near Birmingham, Alabama.

Visit us at
www.historypress.com

....